a Life of Spice

Raksha's story

by Anita Sharma-James

Published in Great Britain in 2011
by Anita Sharma-James
10 Westminster Close
Bromsgrove,
Worcestershire
B61 7PP
www.thespicetrade.com

Photography
Nicole Hynek and Michael Inch

Photograph Restoration
Nicole Hynek

Designer and illustrator
Anthony Ruddy

Food and Props Styling
Carol Mason

ISBN 978-0-9569353-0-4

contents

6

foreword

We each have a story to tell of our culinary and food experiences, and this culinary history also, in ways, charts our life journey. Food footprints, left where we've stopped to cook, and in turn where we've been nourished and revived by others. Food nourishes the body and spirit and for my mother much of her creativity, nurturing and love is expressed in her daily round of cooking. In India, food is as important for its medicinal qualities as for nourishment, with the knowledge of culinary Ayurveda ('knowledge of life') being passed down from generation to generation. My mother is a treasure trove of knowledge about how one can

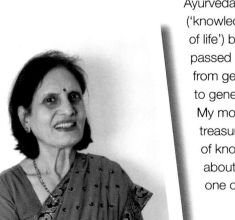

treat a myriad of minor ailments from the contents of her kitchen cupboards and garden beds.

I was born, like my mother, in the Indian State of Punjab. Punjab literally means 'five rivers' and is a rich fertile plain in the North of India, like a vast larder of the subcontinent. A large proportion of the land in Punjab even today, is under cultivation and many locals work in agriculture. Like Britain, the temperate climate in Punjab helps sustain agriculture and has evoked the title 'Bread basket of India'. Punjab produces copious amounts of wheat, sugar cane and milk/diary products. Huge, dark water buffalo are milked by hand and give a rich milk that is used in tea, yoghurt, butter, paneer (whole milk cheese) and ghee (clarified butter).

As a child on visits, I remember cold, misty mornings in Punjab, greeting passers-by faces covered with woollen shawls against the morning chill. Misty mornings with the smell of log fires and cattle dung rising up from every home. Women busying themselves with the domestic chores, shouting

Raksha's story

7

pleasantries across the flat roofs, where spices lay drying and saris billow in the morning sun. Stray, scrawny dogs skulk the alleys, in the hope of finding small bites, as the village comes to life.

I relished the excitement of early morning visits to fields to pick vegetables, and to the village mill to get corn and wheat milled ready for the day's fresh bread. This precious culinary booty was cleaned with well water and turned lovingly into heart-warming dishes that sustain the body and invigorate the mind in equal measure. These are the memories I carry with me, that have travelled with me, from India through my mother and her mother, and a family that have cherished many kitchens.

As I begin to reflect upon my mother's life I realize that what defines her more than anything else is her food and lifelong zeal for creating sublime Indian dishes. So much of her daily life in Britain too, has concentrated on sourcing the best ingredients and preparing and cooking them for the family with great love and attention. The passing of the seasons and Indian Hindu festivals such as Diwali, being marked here, by special dishes reserved only for special times of year. After all, even the Hindu deities are very particular about food, each enjoying favourite offerings. For Krishna, milk and butter are irresistible, whereas Lord Ganesha is very partial to Ladoos, round sweet meats, made with chick pea flour and sugar.

Come with me now on a journey spanning sixty years, several thousand miles, two continents and many glorious dishes along the way.

Dedication

This book is dedicated to my mother,
Raksha, her mother, Yashoda, and
all those who nurture others.

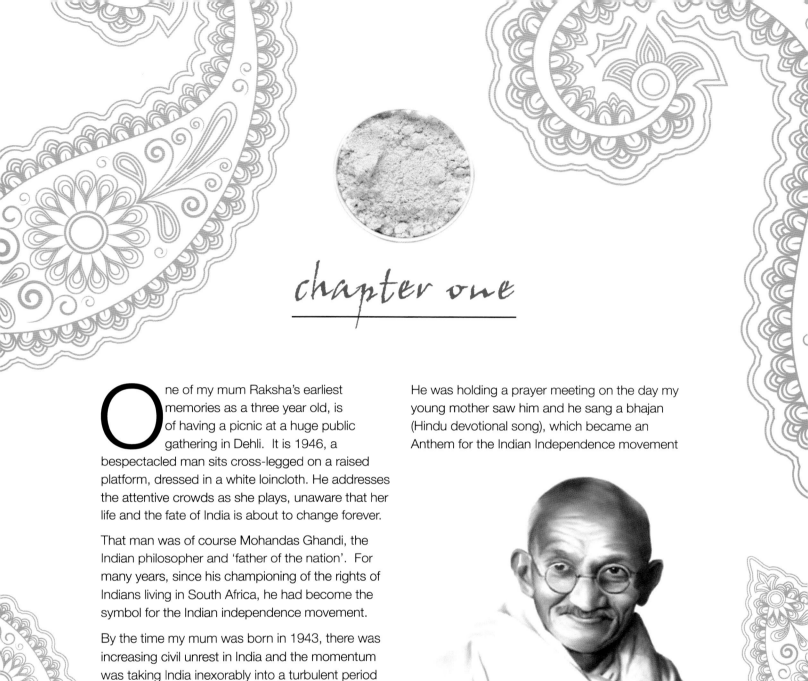

chapter one

O ne of my mum Raksha's earliest memories as a three year old, is of having a picnic at a huge public gathering in Dehli. It is 1946, a bespectacled man sits cross-legged on a raised platform, dressed in a white loincloth. He addresses the attentive crowds as she plays, unaware that her life and the fate of India is about to change forever.

That man was of course Mohandas Ghandi, the Indian philosopher and 'father of the nation'. For many years, since his championing of the rights of Indians living in South Africa, he had become the symbol for the Indian independence movement.

By the time my mum was born in 1943, there was increasing civil unrest in India and the momentum was taking India inexorably into a turbulent period in its history. The British were to leave India as colonial players a year later, leaving behind a mixed legacy which included India being ripped into two parts, divided along religious lines, an outcome that Ghandi had worked hard to prevent .

He was holding a prayer meeting on the day my young mother saw him and he sang a bhajan (Hindu devotional song), which became an Anthem for the Indian Independence movement

A picnic with Ghandi...

and which remained with her, sung at family devotionals, as a school girl and later she would sing the words to her own family.

Ragupati Ragav Raja Ram

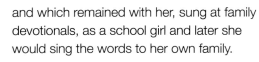

रघुपति राघव राजाराम, पतति पावन सीताराम
सीताराम सीताराम, भज प्यारे तू सीताराम
ईश्वर अल्लाह तेरो नाम, सब को सन्मति दे भगवान

Translation:

Chief of the house of Raghu, Lord Rama,

Uplifters of those who have fallen, Sita and Rama,

Sita and Rama, Sita and Rama,

O beloved, praise Sita and Rama,

Though you are given many names,

All religions have God as one truth at their heart,

Bless everyone with this wisdom, Lord.

In the villages of India eating al fresco is a way of life, with farm workers often eating in the fields. In contrast, Indian city dwellers like my mother's family in Delhi would have made special plans to put together an outdoor banquet. Indian picnics are often held at night when the weather is cooler, under moonlight near a temple, or on the banks of a river. Open air cinema viewings draw huge crowds and are a fabulous excuse for an outdoor Indian meal. Dry curries accompanied by breads as well as fabulous Indian finger food with chutneys, relishes, and dips are perfectly suited for a heavenly outdoor feast.

Vegetable pakoras are perfect to enjoy straight from the picnic basket or sliced inside a delicious wrap together with a thinly sliced leafy salad and spicy chutney. Alternatively drizzle wraps with the heavenly mint and apple relish in the recipe or simply add the raita recipe on page 30. These wraps can be made ahead of time with the sides neatly tucked in, wrapped tighly in waxed paper, and sliced (through the paper) when required- the paper helps to keep them together. The ultimate in mouthwatering Indian picnic experiences.

रघुपति राघव राजाराम,
पतति पावन सीताराम

सीताराम सीताराम, भज प्यारे तू सीताराम

ईश्वर अल्लाह तेरो नाम, सब
को सन्मति दे भगवान

Anita's Vegetable Pakora Recipe (makes 8-10)

Pakoras, a type of bhaji, are versatile gluten-free that can be made using a variety of different vegetables, deep fried in a crispy, spicy batter. They are divine with a fresh mint and apple chutney.

one medium potato (coarse thin slices)

one medium onion (large slices)

Handful of washed spinach leaves chopped coarsely

Approx. 150-200g Gram Flour (chick pea flour or ' besan')

one or two fresh green chillies, (finely chopped) according to taste

one and half teaspoons cumin seeds

1 teaspoon whole coriander seeds (crushed slightly in pestle and mortar)

1 teaspoon salt

2 teaspoons gharam masala

Cold water to mix the batter

Sunflower oil for deep frying

Place the chopped vegetables into a bowl and cover with the gram flour.

Add seeds, spices and chillies to the dry mixture.

Slowly add water to the mixture and mix after each addition until a thick, wet batter (similar consistency to pancake batter) is formed, which binds the vegetables together.

Deep fry large tablespoons of the batter in hot oil (180°c, sufficiently hot for cube of bread to brown in 15 seconds). Cook until the batter turns golden and the vegetables are cooked throughout (approx.7-10mins). Deep fry the pakoras in batches of six, so that the temperature of the oil remains constant. Cooking too many at once will cool the oil. Remove and drain on paper towels. Serve warm whilst still crispy with homemade chutney.

Quick homemade mint chutney

A handful of fresh mint leaves

small chopped onion

one chopped apple

juice of one whole lemon

salt to season

(one de-seeded tomato or chilli-optional)

Blend all ingredients in a small electric blender until the texture is smooth, add salt to taste.

Serve immediately or chill until required.

chapter two

Mum's father, Brahmanand had secured a job with the Indian railway as an accountant in Delhi in 1928. The railways looked after employees from 'cradle to grave' with dedicated hospitals and schools for government workers. He was one of only three men from his home village of Bilga, Punjab, to have been educated, most of his contemporaries worked in the field as agricultural workers or owned little shops in the local bazaar.

The family of six children enjoyed a good living in a part of Old Delhi called Karol Bagh. It was a spiritual vegetarian Hindu upbringing with prayers, meditation and a daily ritual of singing of The Aarti (the Hindu equivalent of the Lord's prayer), every evening at the shrine. Brahmanand had a deep love of music, a harmonium teacher would come to the house to teach him as well as mum's eldest sister Raj.

Mum talks of a highly principled man. A Brahmin family such as theirs was thought to be able to bestow blessings on others so the local people

changes

would gather at house bearing gifts, sweetmeats, and fruits. Brahmanand would never accept these, asking instead that they be taken to the local temple and distributed.

A year after her encounter with Ghandi, mum recalls vividly the traumatic events of the subsequent Indian partition, much of which were felt strongly in Delhi. The houses opposite the family home were looted with people attacked and possessions stolen. Her mother, Yashoda Devi terrified for their safety, hastily collected up all the family's most valuable possessions and her gold jewellery and put them safely in a drawstring sack , which was hidden away.

In the ensuing chaos of the violence and mayhem in Delhi, many public buildings were looted. My mother's eldest brother, Bavaneesh Raman, a bookish intellectual six year old, took a book from the local library in high spirits. Her horrified father sent the boy back to return the book despite the dangers on the streets at the time.

By 1948, a year after Indian Independence was declared, both Ghandi and Brahamanand had died. Ghandi was lost to an assasin's bullet, my grandfather to typhoid fever- he was only 39 years old.

Delhi and the North of India have experienced many invaders and successive dynasties, leaving behind a layered tapestry of cultural and food influences. Today, Delhi is not only the administrative capital of India, but has established itself as the food and restaurant capital of India. The city is teeming with street food, dhabas (open-fronted shops), food bazaars and markets, sweet shops, Tandoori –Mughlai, Punjabi and International restaurants. Delhites just love to eat out. This legacy can be traced back partly to the mass migration and changes brought about by the struggle for Independence and partition.

Up to the time of Independence orthodox Hindus and Brahmins rarely ate food cooked outside the home. The provenance of food and its clean preparation was thought to be greatly important to one's spiritual development. Adulteration of food is regarded, even today, in such circles as one of the worst abuses of another person.

A 'Shudh Brahmin Bhojanalay' (a pure vegetarian eatery), in Old Delhi did not serve any onions or garlic and would have been acceptable places to eat. Certain parantha (stuffed Indian flatbread) shops, such as a few of those found today on Paranthe Wali Gali (literally 'Street of paranthas'), were in the 1940's owned by vegetarian Brahmins. This reference to caste purity in cooking is a true vestige of a bygone era as very few eateries in Delhi today would enquire about the caste of the chef.

A large influx of Punjabis to Delhi fleeing from Pakistan during partition led to the establishment of a new breed of restaurant offering a mixture of Punjabi food and the Mughal cuisine already sold in the old city, prepared by the descendants of royal cooks employed by the Mughal emperors.

The modern day Karol Bagh has bustling markets and boasts many such Punjabi-Muglai restaurants using huge clay tandoor ovens to prepare succulent and creamy dishes.

One of the most popular dishes served by Delhi street food vendors and restaurants alike is chana bhatura. This is a chick pea curry served with a spongy bread, also a firm family favourite and prepared by my mother on special occasions

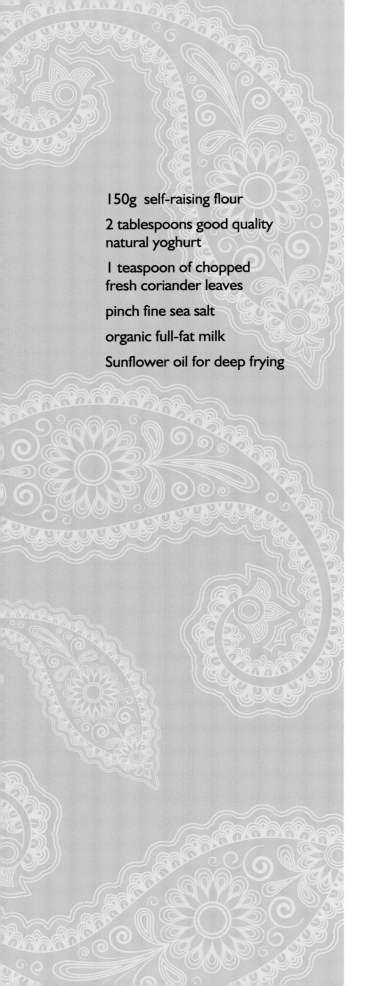

150g self-raising flour

2 tablespoons good quality natural yoghurt

1 teaspoon of chopped fresh coriander leaves

pinch fine sea salt

organic full-fat milk

Sunflower oil for deep frying

Anita's Coriander Bhatura

Add sieved flour to a bowl with the salt and chopped coriander and fold in the yoghurt . Drop-by drop, add sufficient milk to bind the mixture and knead to a firm but elastic dough.

Cover the dough with a damp cloth and leave to relax for 15 mins. Roll out the dough to small ¼ inch thick discs, using SR flour to dust surface. Heat the oil, and deep fry the bhatura for about four minutes, turning regularly, until golden, puffed up and soft.

Drain on kitchen paper.

Serve with curries/dhal/pickles.

Delicious!

Anita's Quick Chana Curry (Chick Pea) (serves 4)

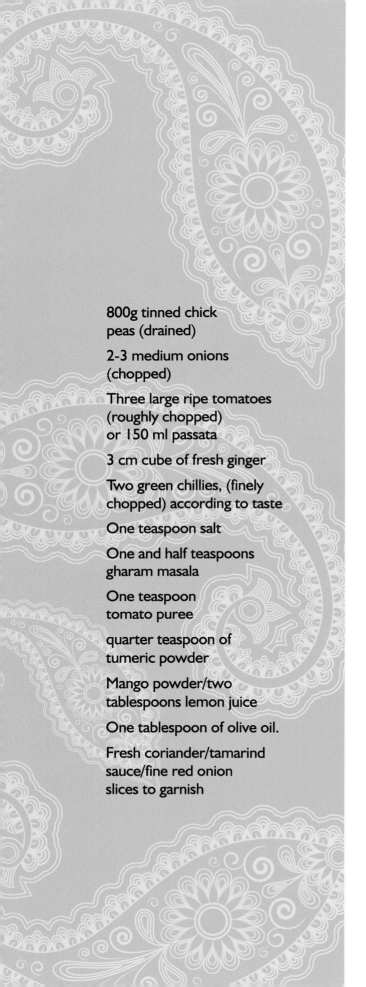

800g tinned chick peas (drained)

2-3 medium onions (chopped)

Three large ripe tomatoes (roughly chopped) or 150 ml passata

3 cm cube of fresh ginger

Two green chillies, (finely chopped) according to taste

One teaspoon salt

One and half teaspoons gharam masala

One teaspoon tomato puree

quarter teaspoon of tumeric powder

Mango powder/two tablespoons lemon juice

One tablespoon of olive oil.

Fresh coriander/tamarind sauce/fine red onion slices to garnish

Heat the oil over medium heat in a deep pan or wok.

Add the cumin seeds and heat until the seeds begin to sizzle.

At this point, add the chopped onion, ginger and chillies fry on low heat unitl they are a golden brown colour.

Stir in the tumeric until this absorbs into the onion mixture, then mix in the tomato puree.

The chopped tomatoes or passata can now go in and cook for a further 5mins, stirring well until the sauce has matured and started to glisten. The gharam masala, salt, mango powder (amb choor) or lemon juice can now be added

To this mixture introduce the chick peas, and 50ml (1/2 cup) water.

Cover and simmer together for 10 minutes on a low heat to let the chick peas absorb the sauce flavours (if further water required during cooking, use boiling water from the kettle).

Turn off the heat and serve garnished with finely sliced onion, natural yoghurt and tamarind sauce. Delicious served with fragrant basmati rice, naan, chapatti or bhatura.

पं: सांई दासजी

(६ दिसंबर १८८९ – १८ दिसंबर १९६५)

chapter three

Mum's Family Tree

Pandit Sai Dassji ── Ishwari Devi

Yashoda Devi ── Brahmanand

Raj (f)
B. 1930
D. 1943

Krishna (f)
B. 1932

Shanti (f)
B. 1938

Bavaneesh Raman (m)
B. 1940

Raksha Devi (f)
B. 1943
(Mum)

Rama Kant (m)
B. 1945

Urmilla (f)
B. 1948

In uncertain times, Yashoda Devi was now left alone with six young children Krishna, Shanti, Raman, Raksha (my mum), Rama Kant and Urmilla, still a babe in arms. With their only means of financial support in the form of her husband Brahmanand cut off, the family returned to Punjab to live with mum's paternal grandparents in the village of Bilga.

Like many Brahmins, Sai Das conducted religious rites for the village Hindu community, prepared astrological charts, and gave advice to locals as a spiritual teacher or Guru. That the course of our lives is influenced by celestial forces is a given in India, with a deep-rooted sense that our souls are part of a wider universe. In all important life decisions (and often even more trivial ones), an astrologer is consulted. Whereas in the West astrology is generally regarded as no more than a distraction, in India the advice given by revered astrologers is carefully heeded and has a deep spiritual significance in life's journey. More often than not the astrologer is a Hindu scholar or Brahmin versed in this ancient Vedic tradition

Back to the Bread basket

On arrival at school the day started with the singing of the Indian national anthem. Originally penned by Rabindranath Tagore in 1911, but later revised and adopted for the newly formed Independent India to unify the diverse peoples of this vast sub-continent.

Indian National Anthem

Jana-gana-mana-adhinayaka, jaya he

 Bharata-bhagya-vidhata

Punjab-Sindhu-Gujarata-Maratha-

Dravida-Utkala-Banga

Vindhya-Himachala-Yamuna-Ganga

Uchchala-Jaladhi-taranga

Tava shubha name jage

Tava shubha ashish maange

Gahe tava jaya-gatha

Jana-gana-mangala-dayaka jaya he

Bharata-bhagya-vidhata

Jaya he, jaya he, jaya he

Jaya jaya jaya, jaya he !

and so it was with my great-grandfather, Pandit Sai Das. The family quickly settled into village life with my him as the head of the household.

Life in rural Punjab was lived very much in balance with nature and its seasonal cycles. Irrespective of the time of year, people tend to go to sleep when it becomes dark and rise with the sun. The year is marked with the cultural splendour and colour of festivals and feast days.

Routinely, Sai Das would wake at 4am meditate and pray for two hours and then bathe before all the family sat down together after breakfast for devotional singing. The children would then leave for school, armed with tiffin boxes. Mum talks of these childhood memories with great fondness, as a time of innocence, in idyllic rural surroundings.

Translation:

Thou art the rulers of the minds of all people,

Dispenser of India's destiny.

Thy name rouses the hearts of Punjab,
Sind, Gujarat and Maratha,

Of the Dravida and Orissa and Bengal;

It echoes in the hills of the Vindhyas and
Himalayas, Mingles in the music of Yamuna
and Ganga and is chanted by,

The waves of the Indian Sea.

They pray for thy blessings and sing thy praise.

The saving of all people waits in thy hand,

thou dispenser of India's destiny,

Victory, victory, victory to thee.

The anthem served to bond the school children
from different religious backgrounds and was
followed by morning lessons in Hindi, Punjabi,
Maths, English and Indian history. Mum was a
compulsive giggler, often being admonished for
outbursts of uncontrollable laughter in class.

On one occasion, her hysterical fits led to a
slap from her teacher and banishment from the
classroom. Instead of standing in the school
courtyard as instructed, my mum decided

that she would not endure
further humiliation and walked home.

As well as picking up culinary skills from home,
school cookery lessons were a compulsory part
of school life, and her younger brother Rama
Kant would carry the heavy fresh produce as
far as the school gates. One of the highlights
of the school day was opening the tiffin
boxes at lunchtime. Each tiffin compartment
contained its own delights, with mouthwatering
subzis (vegetable curries) dhals (spicy lentils),
rotis (Indian flatbreads), pickles and rice.

Fenugreek (methi or 'greek hay') is a Mediterranean herb that is widely used in India. The leaves are nutritious and very slightly bitter, packed with protein and iron and are useful in controlling blood sugar levels. Punjabis use both fresh and dried fenugreek in curries, breads and starters. Fresh fenugreek is available all year round at Indian grocers in bunches. Use the leaves and tender upper stems for this fantastic spicy dry fenugreek and potato salad. Enjoy with raita and Indian breads such as chapatti, makkai ki roti bhatura or puris.

600g new potatoes

300g fresh fenugreek leaves and tender stems

1-2 green chillies, (finely chopped) according to taste

salt to taste

half teaspoon of tumeric powder

half teaspoon of ground black pepper

2 tablespoons of sunflower/ mild olive oil.

Anita's Aloo Methi (spicy dry fresh fenugreek and potato salad) (serves 8)

Wash the potatoes, cut into 1.5 cm cubes and set aside.

Wash the fenugreek leaves and stems in cold water, drain and slice thinly into shreds.

Heat 2 tbsp oil over medium heat in a wide heavy bottomed pan or wok.

Add the tumeric, pepper and chilli and wait 30 seconds then add the chopped fenugreek and stir to coat in the spicy oil.

Stir fry the fenugreek for 1 minute then add the potatoes and salt to taste.

Mix thoroughly and cover to cook for 10- 15 mins on a low heat. Stir every few mins and add a little boiling water from the kettle to prevent sticking if necessary, towards the end of cooking.

Delicious served with a raita and either rice or breads such as chapattis.

These Punjabi corn chapattis are made with **Corn meal or polenta, on a tawa (flat griddle pan).**

Corn is great for those who suffer from a gluten intolerance and is a relatively high protein grain. My mum often had them for breakfast with some natural homemade yoghurt or a raita

500g fine corn meal

150g fresh finely chopped fenugreek leaves (optional)

salt to taste

2 tablespoons of ghee

400ml natural yoghurt

1 finely chopped small red onion

half tsp of finely chopped chilli (optional)

dry roasted cumin seeds

1 teaspoon of fresh chopped mint leaves

1tsp of gharam masala

salt to taste

Makkai Ki Roti (Serves 6)

Boil the kettle and allow the water to cool very slightly.

Sift the corn meal into a bowl. Add one tablespoon of Ghee, the chopped fenugreek leaves and a pinch of salt to taste.

Make a stiff dough with the addition of small amounts of very hot water using a utensil to mix in the first instance, until the dough cools sufficiently to handle. With the warm dough, divide into large balls the size of an apple, and with wet hands shape each ball into a thick disc between your two outspread palms. Alternatively lay the corn disc onto a slightly floured board and rotate the disc with a wet palm, pressing down carefully until it is approximately uniform thickness- about a centimetre thick. You may need to wet your hand repeatedly as you go.

Heat the griddle (tawa) or no-stick dry frying pan until hot, turn down the heat and lay your polenta disc flat onto the disc, cooking both sides on a low heat. This will take at least a minute on each side and will vary depending on the thickness of your disc and your pan. If desired, brush each with the remaning ghee turning over on the griddle to finish off.

Anita's Fresh Raita Dip

In a heated dry frying pan, gently roast the cumin seeds until they darken.

Add the seeds to the yoghurt in a small bowl, and mix in the remaining ingredients

Garnish with a few coriander leaves and a sprinkle of gharam masala/parpika.

Serve in a small relish bowl as a dip or as an accompaniment to a curry with bread.

chapter four

Diwali or 'Deepawali' is one of the great festivals of India, celebrated with great enthusiasm and fervor throughout the country by people of many faiths. It also now marks the beginning of the Hindu New Year. No surprise then that my mother has vivid and colourful memories of this most joyous of Indian national celebrations. The occasion sees the spring-cleaning and white-washing of homes inside and out, decorative designs or rangolis painted on floors and walls to greet the new year.

The Hindu goddess Laxmi, symbolising prosperity and good luck, is thought to visit homes that are brightly lit, and after sunset special prayers and thanks are offered to Laxmi (Laxmi pujan). The lighting of the lamps is also a way for people to show thanks for the good things in their lives.

Although each region of India celebrates Diwali in its own way, the lighting of many small earthenware oil lamps is common throughout the country. The lamps are symbolic of the victory of the light of goodness and knowledge over the darkness of evil and ignorance. Virtue and knowledge is embodied in the legendary Lord Ram, the incarnation of Lord Vishnu and ruler of Ayodhya.

Celebrations start some twenty days before Diwali, upon the day of Dussehra.

On this day, Ram slays the great demon Ravan who has abducted his wife Sita and fled with her to his kingdom of Lanka. Ram, along with his brother Lakshman and devoted follower Hanuman, not to mention an army of monkeys, fight a great ten-day battle to rescue his lovely wife Sita.

Diwali falls each year exactly 20 days after Dussehra on a new moon, in late October or early November. Diwali day itself commemorates the triumphant return of Ram, Sita and Lakshman to Ayodhya after a period of fourteen years exile.

Diwali days

Children make 'deeps' which are small clay lamps to light and usher Laxmi to their home so they can receive new clothes and toys. The first day of Diwali is also a new fiscal year for the business community. All companies pay off debts and their vehicles are decorated with flowers and palm leaves to ensure they run well into the New Year.

Just as with Christmas in Britain, every region and home has it's own way of celebrating Diwali

In mum's childhood home in Bilga, a thorough spring clean would start early morning, with no corner left unturned until the whole house gleamed. This would have followed a white wash of the walls inside and out, a time of renewal to anticipate with optimism, the beginning of a new year. In the late afternoon, divas were lit all round the house in windows and outside the houses on sills, walls and niches. Quite apart from the sprucing and decorating, mum's home was also a flurry of culinary activity on Diwali. The very best fresh produce would have been chosen from the local fields and village bazaar in readiness for the feasting.

The giving and eating of mathai or Indian sweets conveys gratitude, affection and joy. As such, sweets form an integral part of Diwali, whether as an offering at the temple, family shrine, part of a celebratory meal or as a present for family and friends.

Yashoda, with the help of her daughters would spend the day making ladoos (succulent gram flour sweetmeats) using ghee and buying Indian confections such as barfi and jalebis from the local halwai (sweetmaker) in the village bazaar. After sunset, the family would gather to give thanks at the family temple shrine with a special Laxmi Puja. This was followed by hearty feasting, and fireworks being released from the flat rooftops. Deep into the night the whole village would twinkle from the light of thousands of tiny lamps, signifying hope for a bright future.

Fast days and feast days came and went in Bilga, with mum enjoying a sheltered upbringing at a fee paying girls' school. She had a great talent for singing, and was asked to give a private performance for the headmistress in her office every day after lunch. Songs that she was requested to sing included those from the classic 1940's and 1950's era of Bollywood, in addition to more classical devotional songs or bhajans. Indian cinema had a profound influence on the growing Raksha, providing iconic fashion and musical references, with the soundtrack of the latest movies aired weekly, and heard on transistor radios.

She left at the age of 14 having excelled in her 8th Grade exam (equivalent to GCSE's) in Flore, Punjab. Upper schools in Bilga were co-educational, which was regarded by her family as unsuitable. However, so determined was my mother to further her education, that she self taught to metriculation ('A' Level stage) in English, Hindi and Maths in one year. Usually this course would take two years, and she successfully completed the

10th grade exam at 16 years old in Noor Mahal.

She then bought books for a Hindi Bachelor of Arts Degree and began a distance learning course that was never to be completed. Instead, a long trip to the state of Rajasthan was planned that would prove to be both an educational experience, and inform her future.

The house in Bilga still exists and has been rebuilt recently by Rama Kant in honour of Yashoda Devi, Brahmanand and Pandit Sai Dass.

Yashoda, remained in Bilga long after most of the children had emigrated to the four corners of the globe, three daughters to Canada, Kenya and Britain.

The remaining daughter, Shanti, and her two sons (Raman and Rama Kant) settled in India.

These are made on special ocassions and were a favourite on Diwali days.

These dumplings have a wonderful nutty texture, which is beautiful contrasted by the smooth yoghurt. Serve as starter or as an accompaniment to very own special occasion or Diwali day. Yummy!

100g urid dhal (lentils without husk)

50 g mung dhal (lentils without husk)

2.5 cm cube of fresh ginger root (grated)

2 finely chopped chillies (optional)

400ml Natural yoghurt

1tsp of dry roasted cumin seeds

a handful of fresh chopped coriander leaves

salt to taste

sunflower oil for deep frying.

Anita's Dahi Wada (Savoury Lentil Dumplings in Yoghurt)

Wash the dhal and leave to soak in a pan overnight or for at least 3 hours.

Blend the drained urid and moong dhal with a little cold water to make a very thick paste.

Turn out the lentil paste into a mixing bowl, add the grated fresh ginger, chopped chillies and salt. Mix thorougly and then using your hands roll a tablespoon of mixture at a time into a small ball and flatten slightly.

Heat the oil in a wide heavy bottomed pan to a temperature of about 180°c. Carefully deep fry the wada until golden brown and cooked throughout. This should take about 5 minutes on a medium heat. Remove the golden dumplings or wadas onto kitchen paper and set aside to cool. When cooled, soak the fried wadas in a bowl of warm water for about 3 minutes. Gently squeeze out all the excess water from each wada and place in a flat serving dish.

Meanwhile, gently roast the cumin seeds until they darken. Add the seeds to the yoghurt in a small bowl and mix well.

Pour the yoghurt over the lentil dumplings and garnish with a few coriander leaves, a sprinkle of gharam masala or paprika.

chapter five

At the age of 17 years, Raksha travelled with Raman and her grandmother to Bikaner, to the arid desert state of Rajasthan. This family adventure was to have a profound influence on the young Raksha, and start a lifelong association with its regal capital, Jaipur, as both her brothers were to settle there.

Raman had been offered a job in a bank in Bikaner having been previously working in the Dept of Education in Bikaner University. Despite there being many applicants, Raman had secured the post, and went on a pilgrimage to Mata Chintpurni Temple to give thanks, as is customary in India. He was to go on to hold high office in the Rajasthan state bank until his retirement, settling in Jaipur.

Raksha's grandmother's sister and children lived in Bikaner and encouraged her to accompany her grandmother there for a long stay. Soon after their arrival, the heavens opened in a rare downpour in this desert state of Rajasthan. The Rajasthani locals joked that the Punjabi visitors had obviously bought the rain with them from their fertile, lush, plains.

One of the most vibrant aspects of Rajasthani culture is the puppet plays, and mum recalls being mesmerised by the spectacle during her stay. The art of Kathputli ('kath' wood, 'putli' puppets) originated a thousand years ago, when the Bhat community were patronised by royal families in the state. It's popularity grew, with the shows providing moral and social education as well as a compelling form of entertainment. Popular legendary stories are even today enacted by beautiful handmade puppets and performed to the folk music of Rajasthan. The puppets are considered by the Bhats as a type of divinity giving them a livelihood, activity, peace and joy. The magical puppets are handcrafted in areas of Rajasthan such as Udaipur.

Rama kant had started a medical degree at Bikaner University some months earlier. He was later to leave two years into the five year course and set up his own business, becoming an extremely successful entrepreneur based in Jaipur, where he still lives today with his family.

Having experienced something of the possibilities that a large city and university education could offer, mum had hoped that she too would have the

Trip to Rajasthan

opportunity to study in Bikaner, at the University. However, her grandfather did not approve of these aspirations, with very few women going on to study in higher education in India at the time. Those having jobs before marriage would commonly give up their careers to concentrate on the serious business of keeping house and child rearing. Girls were raised to become proficient in all the household skills that may be required once they were married and living with their husbands in a new extended family.

On her return to Bilga, Raksha, with her dreams of a University education thwarted, embarked upon a year-long Arts and Crafts course in embroidery and needlework. Throughout her youth, mum enjoyed a creative flair for making fashionable garments and embroidery. In later years she would use these skills to make clothes for her own family. The course enabled her to start teaching at a nearby Girls' College in the nearby village of Pratapara, making the 5 mile daily journey to the college on her push bike.

Plans were soon afoot to find a suitable husband for my mother. The marriage would be arranged according to custom, from within the caste of

Brahmins. A well-respected photographer in the prestigious city of Lndhiama, was given the responsibility of capturing the all important images that would then be presented to prospective suitors. The matching of couples was meticulously researched so that astrological charts were prepared to check compatibility and Brahmin family 'gotras' (unique family names) analysed, to ensure there was no common ancestry for at least three generations.

Finally, a suitable boy was found, and a message was sent to the family by the prospective in-laws, that it was no longer appropriate for her to be working, mum was 22 years old.

chapter six

The Wedding

It is said that marriages are made in heaven and in India a widespread belief in reincarnation means that Hindu marriages are regarded as the reunion of two separated divine souls, indeed the couple are thought to arrive for the wedding as deities in human form.

So it was that the wedding of my parents, Raksha and Rajinder was arranged by the families, consideration have been given to gotra (family lineage), caste, social standing and the physical attributes of the couple. The nearest best date for the wedding, based on the astrological profile of the couple was thought to be 26th January, 1966. The pair had never seen each other before the wedding day, relying simply on photographs exchanged during the match-making process.

Many people believe that arranged marriage is the traditional form of marriage in India and that romantic marriages are a modern form adopted by a few couples, usually in urban areas. However, there are numerous instances from ancient scriptures in Hinduism of romantic, love marriages being accepted. Somewhere in the course of recent history, arranged marriages became the social norm and the vast majority of Indians today continue to have arranged marriages.

Indian weddings are mammoth undertakings and there now followed several months of careful preparation, which would culminate in three days of ancient wedding ritual, pageant and feasting. Matrimonial details were pored over by family elders on both sides, with a marriage forging deep alliances between families and thereby enhancing social cohesion within caste communities.

The ritual itself is called 'samskara' and was conducted in Sanskrit, the language of ancient North India and Hinduism, by a Pandit scholar (priest). The Sanskrit word for marriage is vivaha, which literally means 'what supports or carries.'

On the wedding day, the baraat (groom's procession) arrives with the groom on horseback, accompanied by the playing of

auspicious shenai, an ancient oboe-like instrument. The groom is welcomed by the bride's family and a blessing in the form of a red tilaka, is placed on his forehead, signifying the Lord's blessing upon him. During this milni (meeting), members of each of the two families get to meet their opposite numbers. For example the two maternal uncles will meet and exchange gifts. The groom is then led to the wedding canopy (mandapa) under which the ceremony will take place.

For spiritual purposes, the groom is given a final opportunity to leave before the bride enters. He is asked if he would like to abandon worldly life and lead the life of an ascetic.

The priest invites the bride to enter and the bride and groom will shower each other with rice. The rice represents prosperity, but is also said to establish dominance in the marriage. The person who throws the rice first will be the most authoritative in the marriage!

The bride and groom exchange beautiful flower garlands (jaya mala) signifying their acceptance of each other. This is highly symbolic, as in ancient times, princesses used to choose from amongst a group of suitors by placing a garland around the preferred suitor's neck.

The wedding ceremony proper begins with the worship of Shri Ganesha, the remover of all obstacles and provider of good luck. All traditional Hindu ceremonies begin with invocation of Ganesha and pujas are also performed evoking the presence of other divine forms to preside over the wedding ceremony.

An Important part of the ceremony is to light a sacred fire in the presence of the bride and groom using ghee (clarified butter) to evoke the great messenger of the Gods, Agnideva the fire God, to witness the proceedings. Throughout the ceremony, the bride, groom and the priest add ghee to the fire to keep it burning. Rice and other sacred ingredients are also added to the fire.

Together we will:

Share in the responsibility of the home

Fill our hearts with strength and courage

Prosper and share our worldly goods

Fill our hearts with love, peace, happiness, and spiritual values

Be blessed with loving children

Attain self-restraint and longevity

Be best friends and eternal partners

With each step they throw rice into the fire, representing prosperity in their new life together.

The highlight is 'Saptapadi' where the bride and groom are linked and take seven steps together around the fire, symbolizing the beginning of their journey through life as partners.

Indian weddings are costly affairs with families saving for many years to cover the costs of the gold jewellery, rich silks and household goods that are presented to the bride and her new family.

Being the eldest son, my dad's family also went to great lengths to make the occasion very special, arriving in a convoy of cars decorated with flowers, at a time when cars were very rare in rural India.

Mum's family sought out the best available halwai (sweet maker and chef) from the nearby town of Nakordur, to prepare the wedding feast. The success of the wedding is often judged by the quality of the food served, so the halwais are under enormous pressure to prepare a banquet for hundreds fit for the occasion.

Hundreds were served in several sittings over the course of the wedding, beginning with tea for the groom's party on arrival. It is customary for the groom's family and guests to be fed first followed by the bride's side. My mum reminds me as we look over the wedding pictures, that copious amounts of alcohol were consumed by the groom's party, although dad's family were believed to be teetotalers!

Halva is a 'catch-all' phrase for an amazingly diverse range of confections and puddings prepared across the Middle East, Eastern Europe, and Asia.

The word is derived from the Arabic 'Halwa' meaning sweet. In each country where Halva is prepared and eaten, there is a special cultural story associated with it, often involving a celebration. It is a universal truth that in times of celebration we turn to all things sweet! This is certainly true of India, where sweets are used in pujas to give blessings, honour deities in temples, given as presents to celebrate important life events and generally sweeten the road ahead. It's not surprising then that numerous different forms of halva are enjoyed in India, including Suji (semolina) halva, aate ka (wheat) halva, mung (mung lentil) dhal halva and gager ka (carrot) halva.

I have included a recipe for semolina halva later in the book. Mung dhal halva was served at my parents wedding and this recipe is a traditional way of preparing this dish that shouts 'congratulations!'

Anita's Mung Dhal Halva

100g (1/2 cup) split mung dhal washed and soaked for 1 hour.

30g (2tbsp) ghee or butter

60g brown sugar or jaggery

½ tsp ground green cardamom seeds

1tbsp finely chopped pistachios

1 tbsp finely chopped cashew nuts

100ml water

Put the water in a pan and add the sugar/jaggery stirring until completely dissolved. Bring this sugar stock to the boil rapidly and allow to simmer on a medium/high heat for 5 mins and then carefully set aside.

Drain the washed mung dhal and blend into a rough paste using a small electric blender.

Heat the ghee/butter in a heavy bottomed pan and stir in the mung paste. Cook on a medium heat until the paste turns a lovely golden brown colour.

Add the hot sugar syrup to the paste, a little at a time stirring vigorously until the mixture begins to thicken. Add the ground cardamoms and remove the halva from the heat.

Serve hot in bowls garnished with the chopped nuts.

Delicious.

chapter seven

As she has done so many times throughout her life, my mother now had to adapt to a completely new way of life, in this case with a new husband and family. Sons typically remained with their parents after marriage, especially in rural communities, and the daughter-in-law joined the household in an extended family arrangement.

As there was already a Raksha in the family, to avoid confusion, it was decided that my mother would be called Sangeeta, by her in-laws.

After a short time on honeymoon, where the couple would begin to get to know each other, my parents settled into life at the home of my paternal grandfather, Sadhu Ram Sharma, in the rural Punjabi village of Kala Sanghian. They shared it with my dad's younger siblings, his parents and grandparents. The house was like many in the Punjab, a three-storey stone house with an open verandha on the middle storey, and a flat roof.

The roofs, along with the village well, bazaar and temple, formed the focal point of life for the village inhabitants. In the mornings, misty in the winter, women busy themselves with domestic chores and shout pleasantries across the roofs and children hail their friends for play. It is often possible to hop across several rooftops before having to scale any dangerously wide gaps.

As well as meeting places for family members, the roofs are used for drying clothes, laying out washed spices in

The Wrong Name

the sun, sewing, flying kites and releasing fireworks, basking in the sun, preparing vegetables for meals, and sleeping under the stars in hot weather.

From the roof one could also enjoy the view of lush open fields surrounding the village, where cereals, fruit and vegetables abound. The majority of land in Punjab

even today is under cultivation and many work in agriculture. Like Britain, the temperate climate in Punjab helps sustain agriculture and has evoked the title ' Bread basket of India.'

People living in India are in the main vegetarian. Cows (or ghai), in particular are cherished for their ability to produce milk, a valuable source of protein and are revered for nourishing us when a mother's milk may not be available. Huge dark buffalo are milked by hand and

50

give a rich milk which is carefully turned into butter (makhan), ghee, yoghurt, and paneer (a young wholemilk cheese). Punjabis often lead very physically active lives and the relative cold, especially in the winter months calls for warming and hearty dishes. Indeed, one of the spice blends used widely in the cooking of the North is gharam masala meaning warming blend. This contains many of the warming spices such as cinnamon, cloves and black pepper that we may use in mulled wines or Christmas tea in mid-winter.

I, Miss SURJEVAN LATA daughter of Mr. Rajinder Pal Sharma whose permanent address in India is Vopo Kala Sanghian Distt Kapurthala India and who is now living at 92 Metchley Lane Harborne Birmingham 17 hereby give notice of my intention to change my name to Anita Sharma subject to the approval of the High Commission of India London.

SIGNED by the said SURJEVAN LATA in)   Signature ..Anita.s.harma
the presence of :-   )   Date.27th...November.1973

SCADDING JESSOP & CO.
SOLICITORS
50 FREDERICK ROAD,
EDGBASTON, BIRMINGHAM, 15

The Daily Telegraph.
26-2-1974

I was born on 18th November, 1966 at the village house in Kala Sanghian, the eldest child of Rajinder Sharma and Raksha Devi. A few days after I arrived, an uncle was entrusted with the job of registering the birth with the registry office in the nearby town of Jalandhar. He duly arrived and when asked the name of the female child to be registered realized that he had forgotten to ask for a name. The uncle thought better of making the long journey back to the village to check the name with the parents and instead registered me on the birth certificate as Surjevan Lata. It was only on his return that the uncle's audacious decision came to light. It's fair to say that his choice of name was not popular with my mother, who resolved that I would be called Anita. It wasn't until 1973 that my name would be legally changed back to Anita.

Pulses and lentils form an enormously important part of the diet of Indians. They are packed with essential proteins, are high in fibre and also contain large quantities of vitamins and minerals.

Black eye beans have a creamy quality, which marries deliciously with the cinnamon and spicy tomato sauce in this recipe.

800g tinned black eye beans (drained and rinsed)

2 medium onions (chopped)

Three large ripe tomatoes (finely chopped) or 150 ml passata

3 cm cube of fresh ginger

Two green chillies, (finely chopped) according to taste

3 sticks of cassia (cinnamon)

5 or 6 whole black peppercorns

1 tsp of cumin seeds

One and half teaspoons gharam masala

2 teaspoons of tomato puree

quarter teaspoon of tumeric powder

One tablespoon of olive oil.

Fresh coriander to garnish

Salt to taste

Anita's Black Eye Bean Curry (Lobia or Rongi)

Heat the oil over medium heat in a deep pan or wok.

Add the peppercorns, cassia and cumin seeds and heat until the whole spices begin to sizzle.

At this point, add the chopped onion and ginger and fry on low heat until they turn golden brown colour. Now add the chopped chillies, stir in, togther with the tumeric, wait 30 seconds, then mix in the tomato puree.

The chopped tomatoes or passata can now go in and cook for a further 5mins, stirring well until the sauce has matured and started to glisten. Season the tarka (spicy paste mixture) with the gharam masala and salt.

To this mixture introduce the black eye beans and stir well, then pour in 100ml of hot water from the kettle. Bring to the boil, then down to a medium heat and simmer for 10 minutes, to allow the beans absorb the sauce flavours. Add extra water if required to get the sauce to the desired consistency.

A fabulous hearty dish, serve with fragrant basmati rice, naan, or chapatti. As a variation on this curry try adding chopped peppers to the spicy sauce and cooking for 5 mins before adding the beans.

The perfect dish for a cold evening!

chapter eight

I had spent the first four months of my life being nurtured by my mother back in Kala Sanghian, Punjab. She recalls leaving me out to play on the verandah and roof and numerous callers to the house taking me for walks around the village. Thus my first sights, sounds and smells, were those of rural Punjab in the Winter. the woodsmoke fires, village wells and bazaar, livestock, the aromatic incense and temple bells.

Rajinder, my father had traveled to England on 26th March, 1966, and was still living in England when I was born. He had spent several years traveling backwards and forwards over the previous five years, working hard in the hope of establishing financial security for his future life. On one famous occasion he and his father, Sadhu Ram made the return journey by ship, a route reminiscent of the early European explorers like Vasco de Gama, around the aptly named Cape of Good Hope. This epic sea journey took six weeks to complete.

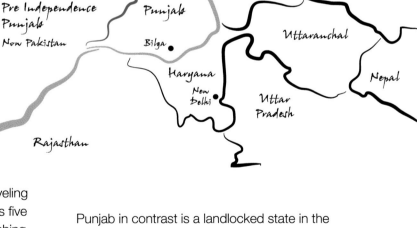

Punjab in contrast is a landlocked state in the northwest corner of India. It is bounded by Pakistan on the west, on the north by Jammu and Kashmir, and by Himachal Pradesh on the

Leap of Faith

Having thought carefully about the opportunities available, it was decided that my father and grandfather would invite the family to relocate to England. They had saved enough money to buy a Victorian semi in a suburb of Birmingham called Harborne.

My mother set to work preparing for her trip with me, still a babe in arms, to England. She had precious little idea of what to expect in this new land thousands of miles away, except for the small amount of news and updates from her husband. She was told that she would need to buy a milk bottle for me, as breastfeeding was not socially acceptable and she was warned about the bitter cold.

east and Haryana and Rajasthan on the south

The partition of India in 1947 and the location of Punjab on the new boundary meant that a large number of refugees from Pakistan came into the Jalandhar area. This increased the pressure on the resources in the State.

We stayed in Dehii briefly before the flight, and mum hurriedly scoured the markets in search of a baby's winter coat, leaving me with her mother. On her return, the purchased coat proved to be a very tight squeeze, but with time running out before the journey, she somehow managed to pull it onto me. Being a mother myself now, I can appreciate more fully the enormous courage it took for my mother to board a plane for the first time in her life, bound for a foreign destination some 5000 miles away, with a four month old baby in her arms. She had no idea at the time when she would be able to return to India to see her family. It was a great leap of faith and expression of hope for the future.

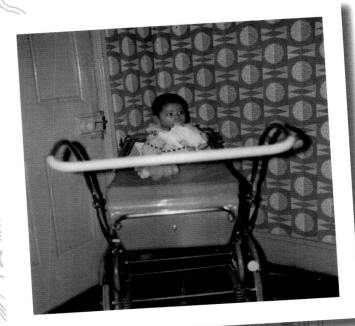

My mother and I touched down with step mother-in-law and three children at London Heathrow on April 6th, 1967, to a snowy landscape. The Delhi winter coat providing valuable protection from the cold. My mum had never seen or experienced snow before, and this added to the sensation of landing somewhere totally other-worldly.

The English spring of 1967 was very late and proved exceptionally wet, following on from a bitterly cold winter. She quickly realised that the outdoor rural life she had been used to would give way to a new suburban life in Birmingham, where most people kept to themselves.

It was difficult to get the fresh Indian produce, herbs and spices she had so taken for granted in Punjab. The family didn't have a car until 1969 but were excited to discover that there was a local grocer about two miles away in Smethwick, who could deliver what was then considered exotic produce such as fresh ginger, chillies,

herbs and spices. A phone call led to an order for the first weekly delivery.

When the delivery arrived mum was disappointed in the lack of freshness and poor quality of the imported produce, hardly surprising for someone who has recently arrived from India's agricultural heart and routinely cooked fresh from the field and village bazaar.

So started a whole new life for my mother and the extended family, gradually acclimatising to a new way of life, language, and culture. As with all those living in non-native lands, the kitchen at the heart of the home provided a vital link to the motherland and through the rich aromas, spice flavours and textures, memories were evoked and souls comforted.

If ever a dish could epitomise and evoke the lush green fields of the state of Punjab, it is Saag. Saag is a fabulous way of cooking armfuls of fresh greens and transforming them into a comforting hot, spicy, puree which can be scooped up with hot chapattis or corn rotis.

1 kg of mixed greens;

mustard tops/ broccoli / spinach washed and sliced into ribbons/fine slices

boiling water

one medium, finely chopped onion

3 green chillies, (finely chopped) according to taste

2tbsp ginger grated

4cm cube of finely chopped ginger

1 teaspoon salt

handful of corn meal

1 tbsp sunflower oil

An electric blender or alternatively lots of arm power!

Mum's Saag recipe (spicy seasonal greens)

Place the chopped greens in a very large heavy bottomed pan and add the boiling water so that the water is just covering the leaves.

Bring the water back to the boil and then turn down to a simmer, making sure that the leaves are immersed in the water.

Add the grated ginger and chillies into the cooking saag and cook for about 30 minutes until the water has largely evaporated. Keep any remaining green water in the pan with the saag. Remove the pan from the heat and allow to cool.

Dry roast the corn meal in a frying pan gently until it is lightly toasted and a lovely corn aroma emanates from the pan. Blend the leafy mixture in small amounts in a blender and return the contents to the pan. Stir in the toasted corn meal and reheat thoroughly until the blended saag begins to leave the sides of the pan.

In another frying pan, add the chopped onions to a tablespoon of the heated sunflower oil and sauté lightly then add the chopped ginger and cook for a couple of minutes. Add this to the heated green saag mixture and season with salt to taste. Gorgeous served with hot flatbreads such as makkai ki roti and chapatti and a raita or lemon pickle (achaar).

Heaven.

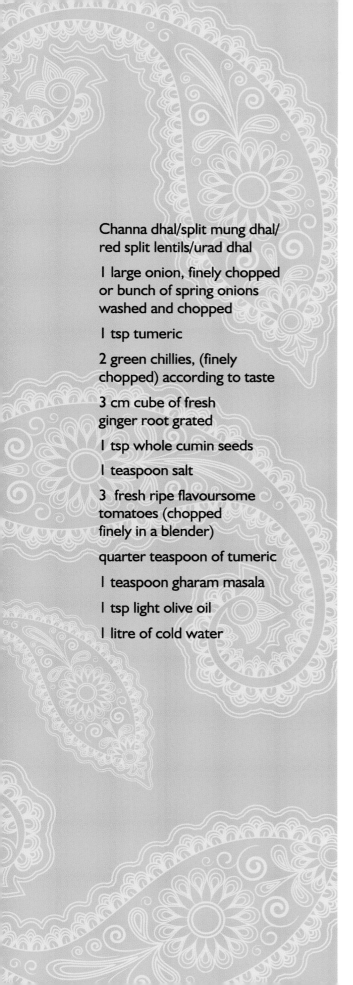

Mum's Spicy Mixed Lentil dhal

Channa dhal/split mung dhal/
red split lentils/urad dhal

1 large onion, finely chopped
or bunch of spring onions
washed and chopped

1 tsp tumeric

2 green chillies, (finely
chopped) according to taste

3 cm cube of fresh
ginger root grated

1 tsp whole cumin seeds

1 teaspoon salt

3 fresh ripe flavoursome
tomatoes (chopped
finely in a blender)

quarter teaspoon of tumeric

1 teaspoon gharam masala

1 tsp light olive oil

1 litre of cold water

Leave the channa dhal to soak for an hour
and mix with the other lentils in a litre of
water. Add tumeric and salt and bring to
the boil. Turn down and when it starts to
simmer, add the grated ginger and chopped
chillies. Cook the lentils in ginger water until
soft enough to crush between fingers.

Heat oil in a heavy bottomed pan. When hot,
add the cumin seeds until they sizzle and turn
a golden brown. Now add the chopped onions
and cook until they become translucent.

Introduce the chopped tomatoes and cook until
the tomatoes and onions are well combined to
form a rich paste. Stir in the gharam masala.

Add this spicy paste mixture to the
cooked lentils and bring back to the boil
mixing thoroughly to allow the paste to
disperse evenly throughout the dhal.

Simmer the dhal for five minutes and serve
hot with chapattis or rice and pickles.

Gharam masala is an aromatic blend of spices with each Indian household having its unique family recipe. The spices used are warming to the body, including cloves, cinnamon, black pepper and black cardamom. Indian bay leaves (or tej patta) is often added to counterbalance the blend by introducing a 'cooling' influence. Masala is generally sprinkled into curries, raitas and savouries to give wonderful depth of flavour and aromas.

40g Coriander Seeds

40g Cumin Seeds

20g Black Peppercorns

5g Casia Bark or cinnamon

10g Black Cardamons

Handful cloves

10g Ground Ginger

Handful of Bay Leaves

Anita's Gharam Masala Recipe

Blend all the above ingredients and then grind the mixture in an electric spice mill/blender.

Store ground masala in an airtight container for six months and use as required.

Chapattis are one of the great staples of the Asian subcontinent. It is a simple flat bread made from flour called atta that can accompany any South Asian dish, especially vegetarian dishes such as dhals (lentil based spicy soups) or sabjis (vegetable based curries). The chapatti has different names in different parts of India. For example in Punjab it is called roti or phulka, in Gujarat it is called rotli and in some areas of Maharashtra it is called poli.

2 cups fine whole wheat flour

cold water

some dry chapatti flour for dusting

Chapattis (Unleavened Indian flatbread)

Place flour in a large bowl and gradually add small amounts of the water as required to bind into a firm dough ball. Knead well for 5mins until the mixture is smooth firm and elastic. Then form a compact ball. Set dough aside for at least 15 minutes to relax.

Make a ball about the size of a golf ball using the palms of your hands. Flatten the ball into a circular shape with your hand and dip both sides into the flour container. Scatter a little flour on a surface and using a rolling pin roll the dough outwards into a circular shape about 1/8inch thick, turning it over as required. Heat a griddle/tawa on a high heat stove (a dry non-stick frying pan can also be used) and then turn down to a medium heat. Put the rolled chapatti on the griddle and allow to cook for about 30 secs.

Turn and cook the second side for a minute until small brown bubbles form. Turn over again and lightly press with a clean tea towel or place onto the flame until the chapatti fills with air.

Remove from tawa/griddle and brush with butter/olive oil if desired.

chapter nine

T he England we had descended upon in late 1960's was a world that had Harold Wilson at the helm as Prime Minister, the Beatles in the charts, where a gallon of petrol cost 5 shillings 2 pence (or 27 new pence) and the average house price was £3,800. At the same time as we had ventured west, there seemed to be a growing interest here and in the US in Eastern philosophies, spurred by protests against the Vietnam war and civil rights abuses.

There were signs everywhere that all was not well with the economy, although my father, Rajinder, and grandfather Sadhu Ram were working hard to try to keep the large family afloat. There was an amazing work ethic amongst the migrant communities of the time, exemplified by my father and grandfather who had bought the Victorian house in Harborne outright, by working long hours and multiple shifts before we had arrived in the country. Emigrants to the UK in the late 1950s and early 1960s were predominantly men, who settled in inner city areas and then were later able to invite their families to join them.

By buying a house in a largely Caucasian suburb of Birmingham, in Harborne, the family was geographically more isolated from the migrant Indian diaspora. The house had high ceilings, draughty sash windows, and a couple of fires, one of which was a mobile paraffin heater which was moved to whichever room most of the family had congregated in for the evening.

In 1969, my younger sister, Suman was born. A few months after her birth, it was decided that my mum should start working in order to help to support the now extended family of nine. Despite her teaching experience in India and her obvious academic ability, she had had little opportunity to improve her conversational English, relying day to day on

East meets West

sometimes was by a gift, but always by the preparation from scratch of a fabulous, comforting Indian meal.

My grandfather, Sadhu Ram loved to be outdoors, a keen farmer and horse breeder, in India, he had an interest in all things natural, especially food.

When he wasn't working, he would often take me out for long walks from the age of three. More often than not, the objective for the day would be to find the best produce for the evening meal. We soon discovered all the best shops for everything from spices to Indian sweets, fresh fruit and vegetables. Unfortunately, few of these shops were within easy walking distance and my little legs were asked to make a return journey of six miles to Smethwick, Bearwood or Handsworth, bearing our precious booty in grandad's large black sack.

On our return we would proudly turn out sackfuls of seasonal English produce, as well as pungent alphonso mangoes, pulses, nuts, exotic vegetables like okra, and fresh herbs, fresh chillies and ginger. Sadhu Ram, like my mother, instilled in me the notion that nothing was more important than eating well. Food was a great joy, a gift from good to be embraced and only loving and mindful, preparation would do it justice.

the school English lessons of her youth. With an imperative to earn some money fast, and therefore little opportunity to seek training for a formal career, she took the route of many migrants before her, taking up a full time job at a factory in Birmingham making packaging and cardboard boxes.

I felt my mother's absence keenly for the first time in my life, as during the day, my sister and I were left with my father's stepmother, Biro, whose two sons and older daughter were all old enough to attend the local school in Harborne. Mum traveled to her workplace in Hockley by bus everyday, and I would eagerly await her return in the evening, accompanied, as it

Anita's Mango Fool
Serves 6

800g fresh mango flesh

300ml full-fat crème fraîche

1 tbsp kirsch

6 tbsp icing sugar

one and a half tbsp lime juice

Cut the fresh mango into small fine pieces. Place the crème fraîche in a large bowl. Whisk until it forms firm peaks, then gradually add the mango. Next, whisk in the kirsch, icing sugar and lime juice to taste. The fool should just hold a trail. Serve in wine goblets garnished with sprig of mint.

Bhindi Masala (Okra/Ladies Fingers)

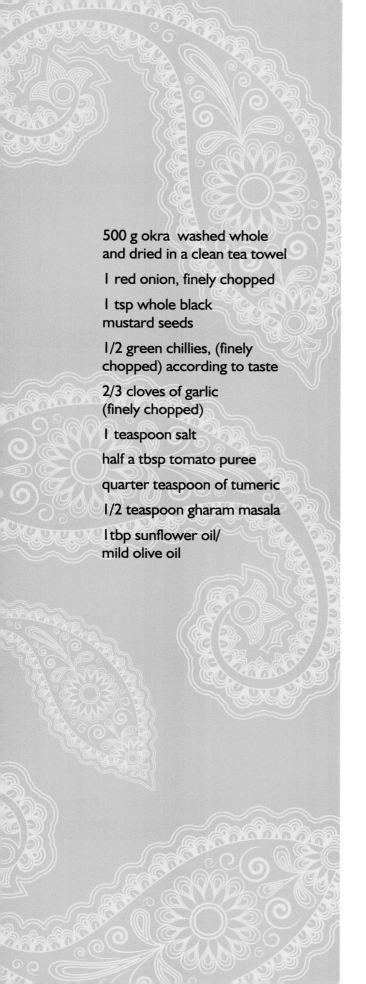

500 g okra washed whole and dried in a clean tea towel

1 red onion, finely chopped

1 tsp whole black mustard seeds

1/2 green chillies, (finely chopped) according to taste

2/3 cloves of garlic (finely chopped)

1 teaspoon salt

half a tbsp tomato puree

quarter teaspoon of tumeric

1/2 teaspoon gharam masala

1 tbp sunflower oil/ mild olive oil

Wash the okra whole and dry completely in a clean tea towel. Top and tail the okra and set aside.

Heat the oil in a heavy bottomed pan/non-stick pan.

Add the mustard seeds until they begin to pop and sizzle and flavour the oil.

Now introduce the chopped red onion/ garlic to the pan and soften and cook until the onions are golden brown.

Add the chopped chillies according to taste, cooking for 30 secs and stir in the tumeric

At this stage the tomato puree can be added to give a thick paste. If necessary take the pan off the heat to prevent sticking and season the paste with the salt and gharam masala.

Stir in the whole okra to the aromatic paste adding a drop of hot water from a boiling kettle every now and again to prevent sticking. Cover and allow the okra to cook for approximately 10-15mins until tender, succulent coated in a spicy sauce. Enjoy! Great as accompaniment to a dhal, or eaten with breads such as chapatti.

This mixed whole bean dhal with black beans (maahn), moth beans and kidney beans (rajma)is slow cooked to create an earthy, creamy dhal of the type that would have graced many a rajah's table.

half cupful of quantities of the moth and blackbeans

a handful of rajma

Cold water for boiling (four volumes of water)

2 green chillies, (finely chopped) according to taste

3 cm cube of fresh ginger root grated

I tsp whole cumin seeds

I teaspoon salt

three fresh ripe flavoursome tomatoes (wizzed in a blender)

I teaspoon gharam masala

I tsp light olive oil/ghee

Mum's Sabat Maahn, moth aur rajma dhal

Bring dhal to the boil with salt turn down and simmer on a medium heat. After 10 mins add grated ginger and chopped chillies. Cover the pan, after 30 mins turn heat to a low heat. Cook lentils for about hour until the lentils are soft between fingers. If the lentils start to thicken too much add a little boiling water from the pan

Heat the oil in a heavy bottomed pan. When hot, add the cumin seeds until they sizzle and turn a golden brown. Now add the blended tomatoes and cook until they are well combined to form a rich paste. Stir in the gharam masala. Add the spicy paste mixture to the cooked lentils and bring back to the boil mixing thoroughly to allow the paste to disperse evenly throughout the dhal.

Simmer the dhal for five minutes and serve with chapattis or rice and lemon/lime achar.

chapter ten

I n 1971, I started school at the local primary, an experience that proved rather a culture shock. I was the only ethnic child at the school, which suddenly made me acutely aware of race differences, something that I had never previously considered. Apart from exchanging pleasantries with neighbours, there was little socializing with the English inhabitants of Harborne village. So started a very steep learning process about English social values and mores of the early 1970s, which were quite different from those of today.

One of the most difficult things to adapt to was the contrast between what passed as a school meal and the scrumptious Indian meals I was served lovingly at home. I was shocked by the indifference of the women in canteens who slopped food carnage onto my plate. There seemed to be a general lack of interest in, and knowledge of, food amongst those who were entrusted with feeding us. When I tried to explain that I was vegetarian I got blank looks and occasional offers of some tinned tuna or boiled eggs. There were no vegetarian options as such, with the only option being to have the translucent boiled cabbage and packet mash that accompanied the meat of the day. Sadly the sweet dishes were no

better, and eventually after many months of pushing the school food around my plate, a member of staff noticed that I hardly ate anything at lunchtime. My parents were called up to the school and lectured about the importance of instilling good eating habits.

The marketing men of the time were selling a food culture of futuristic convenience. We all

remember the adverts depicting alien robots mocking humans that use traditional

Life on Mars

nationwide unrest, with strikes, power cuts, a three-day week and candles being used in the evenings. My routine tonsil removal operation in 1972 became a drawn out affair requiring hospital generators and many cancellations.

In the summer of 1973, my dad's stepsister, Darshana was married and much of the food for the three days of celebration was made at home. Huge cauldrons of steaming subzhis, dhals and succulent sweet gulab jamuns graced every kitchen surface. Extra stockpots full of ghulab jumans were stored in the garden shed, and having a sweet tooth, I sneaked into the shed on several occasions to raid these delights. The wedding provided a very colourful spectacle for the English neighbours in the street who came out of their houses to watch the bridal procession leave the home.

The year after the wedding in 1974, my grandparents and their sons decided to return to India. My grandfather was missing running his farm and livestock in Utrapradesh, which had been managed for him during his stay in the UK.

cooking methods. Instant Whip, Birds custard, and the 'just add water' slogan all set the tone of the times. Whilst these products evoke a sense of nostalgia, they had all the flavour and nutritional content of a 1970's airline meal. Infact they were one small step away from the insipid bars eaten by astronauts on board the Apollo missions which fascinated the public. We were sold the dream of freedom from the 'chore of cooking' but in an Indian family, cooking could never be a chore.

At around the same time, my father had saved enough to buy his first new car, a bottle green Volkswagen beetle. I have vivid memories of going to pick it up with him. On the journey back I stood on the back seat with my arms wrapped round his neck and sensed his excitement and joy, in the way only a child can. Compulsory seatbelts for children were still some years away, which made for some interesting journeys with impossible numbers of occupants in cars.

The early 1970s were a worrying time for my mother, with much coverage in the media of the risk of a nuclear war and endless cold war rhetoric being exchanged between the US and Russians. At home there was

Soon after her in-laws left for India mum decided to stop working. Suman had recently started school and mum wanted to be around to look after us now that the extended family had emigrated. Her incredible thrift and resourcefulness more than made up for the loss of her income. She was now the proud owner of a new sewing machine and she was busy crocheting, knitting and sewing some wonderful 1970s clothes creations for us.

The spring of 1975 ushered in a new baby for my mother to care for, my sister Seema was born in the end of March. In November of the same year, mum and dad planned a three month family trip to India that was to change my life forever. Until that time, although my conscious memories were of England, there was a feeling of separation that I couldn't explain. We travelled extensively all over the north of India staying with Yashoda, mum's mother in Bilga, her brothers, Raman and Rama Kant, in Jaipur, Rajasthan and my dad's parents in the house where I was born in Kala Sanghian, in the Punjab. I recall standing on the rooftop where I had been laid as a baby and looking out over the fields beyond the village. Even as a nine year old I felt overwhelmed by the experience and mindful of the great adventure that my parents had embarked upon. The freedom, colour,

noise and bustle of India was so exciting to me. Among the sensory overload that is India, I experienced an epiphany, a realization of who I was and I returned feeling reconciled that I could belong to both Britain and India at the same time.

We arrived back in UK in the year of a record heat wave and drought, a far cry from the snowy landscape that first greeted us to the UK almost exactly ten years earlier. It was a fantastic summer for a nine year old like me. The dark, grim mood, that had characterized the early 1970s had finally lifted.

The national celebrations to mark the Silver Jubilee in 1977 epitomised a more buoyant and optimistic mood in the nation.

In September of 1977 my youngest sister, Sheetal was born, just as I started at Lordswood Girls' school, a senior school in Harborne that all four of us would pass through.

Mum's Gulab Jamun Recipe

Gulab Jamuns are probably India's favourite desserts often served up at weddings and celebrations. Succulent soft milk dumplings floating in a cardamom and rosewater sugar syrup.

450g (2 cups approximately) full fat milk powder

three handfuls of fine semolina

100g self raising flower

30g (2tbsp) ghee

whole milk

400g sugar

½ tsp ground green cardamom seeds

600ml water

¾ drops of Rose water

Sunflower oil for deep frying

Sieve the milk powder, semolina, and flour into a bowl.

By slowly adding the milk, kneed into a soft dough.

Rub a little ghee into the palm of your hand and roll the dough into round 1 inch balls, applying ghee in between each ball.

Deep fry the dough balls in batches on a gentle heat turning rapidly and continuously to ensure even cooking and colour. Remove from the oil onto kitchen paper. The insides should appear like a spongy lace lattice when the jamuns are removed from the oil and broken. Allow the jamuns to cool while you make the sugar syrup.

Put the water in a pan and add the sugar stirring until completely dissolved, add the ground cardamom and rose water.

Bring this sugar stock to the boil rapidly and allow to simmer on a medium/high heat for 10 mins and then set aside. When the jamuns have cooled, bring the sugar stock

solution back to the boil and when simmering gently add them gently allowing them to absorb the cardamom syrup for two or three minutes, then remove from the heat.

Serve the gulab jamuns warm in bowls garnished with grated coconut.

500g Medium Cauliflower florets coarsely grated

Salt one and a half teaspoons of salt

1 tsp Gharam masala

2 fresh chillies

1 tsp ajwain (carom) seeds

½ tsp dried ginger

dried methi (fenugreek) 2/3tsp

7-8 tbsp gram flour

1tsp cumin seeds

1 blended/grated white onion

4cm cube grated ginger

2-3 finely chopped chillies

1 tin of plum tomatoes or 200ml passata

1tsp gharam masala

½ tsp turmeric

1tsp salt

500ml warm water from kettle

1tbsp light olive oil

Cauliflower Kofta

Add besan/gram flour to the grated cauliflower mix, with no extra water to make a firm dough which binds together well

Roll into 1 inch/2cm diameter balls

and deep fry in sunflower oil. Remove from the oil onto kitchen roll.

Kofta Sauce

Heat oil in a pan. When hot add cumin seeds until they sizzle and become golden brown.

Now introduce the onion ginger and chillies and cook until the onions start to brown. Add the turmeric and passata or tinned tomatoes. Reduce down the tomato sauce until glossy and stir in the gharam masala and season with salt. Add 500ml of water from the kettle.

Bring to the boil and simmer for 20 mins then add kofta and let the sauce come back to the boil and simmer only for three mins.

80

chapter eleven

The 1980s saw the emergence of confident second-generation Indian communities, and with greater integration and cultural exchange, they were increasingly being accepted in Britain. By the end of the decade, Indian food had become the most popular cuisine in the country. This decade also saw the rising power of supermarkets giving ready accessibility to the sort of exotic imported ingredients that my mother had sourced as soon as she had arrived in the UK. This allowed more people to experiment in their own kitchens. At the same time, the widespread use of microwaves spurned a second wave of demand for convenience foods and ready meals.

My parents had started growing their own vegetables and herbs in the modest back garden of their Victorian house. Horseradish, carrots, onions, cabbage, potatoes, coriander and mint were all turned into relishes, pickles, curries, stuffed breads (paranthas) and used for salads. My mum is a treasure trove of information about how one cures minor ailments with foodstuffs from the kitchen cupboards to the herb garden. Much of this information was passed down through Indian families, and has its origins in the ancient Hindu texts of the Vedas. I now use the wisdom mum passed onto to me to treat my own family.

Ayurveda or the knowledge of life, regards food as a vital healing source. By living in sync with the cycles of nature and eating mindfully according to some basic principles, then a state of health should be the natural one for us.

In the mid-1980s I left home to go to university in Nottingham. The culinary skills my mother had passed onto me served me well in student life. While many of my peers survived on pot noodles and very suspect take away meals, I was able to bewilder them by preparing my fresh Indian food, sometimes falling back on simple fusion snacks such as my own version of curried beans on toast !

There has been much cross-fertilisation of the food culture in both directions. Asians have adopted Ketchup to splash onto their samosas and pakoras, while breakfast cereals now mark the start of the day alongside the more traditional paranthas. Pizzas also cried out for adoption and a healthy dose of spices and chillis soon transformed them into a dream for chilli and cheese lovers.

It amuses me that my parents rarely travelled to India from this time onwards, without some muesli or other well-known wheat cereal carefully packed into their super sized suitcases. Indians going abroad are usually very easy to spot by glancing

Back to the Future

at suitcases. Hundreds of eager relatives waiting for clothes, perfumes, and all things English, mean that before a flight travellers are inevitably groaning under the weight of luggage and worrying about whether their weight allowance has been breached.

Rural communities in Punjab and elsewhere in India have benefited enormously from the financial contributions and expertise of family members living in England. Hospitals, water, school and temple building projects to name a few, have all been

made possible by constant nurturing from British Indians like my parents.

My mother continued to nurture her four girls in her myriad ways and we thrived, all going on to University and having professional careers, a teacher (Suman), a pharmacist (Sheetal) and two scientists (myself and Seema).

Three of us are now married, myself included, with children, and the fourth is a jet-setting career woman.

After completing my PhD, I worked for almost ten years as a clinical research scientist in a university setting. Following the birth of my daughter, Anya, I decided to give up my career to look after her.

Without realising it at the time, she was to give me the opportunity to start a whole new life as an entrepreneur. The passion for food that my mum had instilled in me, led me to start an Indian cookery school from the kitchen table. In the early days of the business, my mum was horrified that I was giving up an academic career to teach cookery.

Looking back at my mother's early life, I can understand now that for someone so academically able, being denied the opportunity to complete the degree that she began in the early 1960s, must have frustrated her beyond measure. Watching me give up professional life having had all those opportunities must have been very difficult. Today, after the continuing success of the business and seeing first hand how scores of people are being introduced to her incredible recipes and her knowledge of the health benefits of herbs and spices, she can now see how my knowledge of health and love of food can be expressed together. So the business was born through her, and in some senses through our life journey together, a remarkable pedigree.

My parents have spent much of the time since the sisters left home, travelling, going on pilgrimages all over India, and helping to develop charity projects such as a hospital offering free treatment for polio sufferers and a project that helps to nurture ophans by bringing them up in communal family units.

My mum was able to pursue her life long love of music and took up the harmonium, an Indian keyboard that has bellows attached, so that it is played one-handed. She also started singing again at the Hindu temple and gave many public performances as she had done for her headmistress in her school days. The performances led to mum studying for and completing a music diploma through a community initiative.

Looking to the future, the sacrifices of so many Indian mothers like my own mean that British Indians have emerged as a very successful and integrated immigrant group, excelling in business, finance and academia.

At the same time India is emerging as a growing economy with a reputation for expertise in IT and the sciences and as the world's largest democracy, may help to mould the future for the better.

With a burgeoning middle class there is a growing appetite for new restaurant experiences in India, including Chinese, Thai and Italian. Despite the best efforts of the fast food outlets to break into India, the cultural and religious links to indigenous food and ingredients are so strong that these consistently fail to make much progress.

Of the one billion population of India, around sixty to seventy per cent are vegetarian, making vegetables, pulses and legumes hugely important in the diet to complement the carbohydrate staples of rice and wheat. This makes for a more sustainable way of farming with less water, land, and precious resources having to be directed towards the rearing of animals for meat.

The future of food in this country is also very optimistic with a growing movement to connect with, grow, source and cook local natural, produce.

There is a growing awareness about the important link between health, food and well being. Cookery has become the new rock and roll, with celebrity chefs and wall-to-wall cookery programmes gracing our screens. The restaurant culture in Britain has blossomed since the relative culinary gloom of our arrival in the 1960s and offers a dizzying array of choice when it comes to fabulous award-winning restaurants and eateries.

No wonder my mum is still smiling......

This is simple but satisfying tangy gram flour and yoghurt soup. To make it more substantial you can add some par boiled potatoes half way through simmering the soup they will then be perfectly cooked when the soup is ready.

1 1/2 cups thick plain yoghurt

4 tblsp gram flour (besan)

750 ml cold water (3cups)

1 tbsp olive oil

1tsp fenugreek seeds

2 tsp black mustard seeds

6 curry leaves chopped

3 garlic cloves finely chopped

1 teaspoon ground tumeric

1 tsp finely chopped chilli

1 small onion finely chopped

salt to taste

Anita's Karhee

In a bowl or jug mix together the yoghurt, sieved gram flour, and 750ml water to a smooth liquid. Heat the oil a deep pan over a low heat. Introduce the mustard and fenugreek seeds, and the curry leaves. Leave for a minute until they begin to sizzle. Now add the onion and cook until soft and beginning to brown. Introduce the garlic and stir in, allow to cook for one minute. Now add the ground tumeric and chopped chilli and stir for 30 secs. Gently and carefully pour in the yoghurt and gram flour mixture, bring to the boil and simmer over a low heat for approximately 20 mins until golden and creamy with a lovely shine.

Season with plenty of salt to taste.

Suji or semolina halva was often cooked by my mum as nourishing sweet breakfast on days when we were not at school or in the late afternoon to enjoy with tea. It always reminds me of the comforts of home.

200g fine semolina

120g unsalted butter

80g jaggery

120g soft brown sugar

50g ground almonds

50g sultana, raisins or dried cranberries

600-700 ml water

Suji kar Dhal Halva

Put the water in a pan and add the sugar and jaggery stirring continuously until completely dissolved. Bring this sugar stock to the boil rapidly and allow to simmer on a medium/high heat for 5 mins and then carefully set aside.

Melt the butter in a heavy bottomed pan and add the semolina and ground almonds. Stir continuously for about 7-10 mins until the semolina turns a golden brown colour and puffs up in texture. Add the dried fruit and toast slightly with the semolina.

Very carefully, add the hot sugar syrup to the paste, a little at a time stirring vigorously until the mixture begins to thicken. Add the ground cardamoms and remove the halva from the heat. Serve hot in bowls

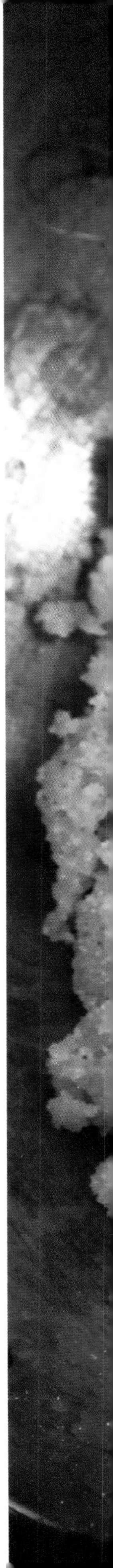

Afterword

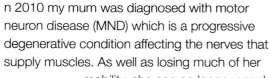

I n 2010 my mum was diagnosed with motor neuron disease (MND) which is a progressive degenerative condition affecting the nerves that supply muscles. As well as losing much of her mobility, she can no longer speak and has to write things down for us. The illness has also affected her ability to swallow. She is now unable to eat many of the meals that she loved so much. In spite of this, she has remained dignified and good-humoured. She still smiles and giggles a lot, as she always has. She continues to cook meals for other people with the same pride and passion she has always had.

My mum's stoical attitude in the face of this illness gave me the inspiration to start writing this book, a tribute to all that she is and the incredible journey that she has made. She instilled in us a deep sense of spirituality, a strong moral compass and an awareness of the sacred nature of good food, the importance of eating mindfully and the supreme joy of feeding others.

The simple act of eating. So easily taken for granted in our busy lives. We would do well to take that little breath of time to say grace, whatever our beliefs, before enjoying the blessed gift of food.

This was my inspiration.
I hope you will be inspired too.

Recipe Index

Acknowledgements

Thanks so much to everyone who has helped to create this book by providing support, inspiration, guidance and practical help.

Mum, Dad Suman, Seema and Sheetal who shared the journey.

Mum thanks for spending time patiently writing out answers to the many questions I had about your early life, even though you were feeling tired at times.

Nicole Hynek, thank you for keeping the flame burning for the project and helping me so much in the early stages with your sensitivity and photography skills.

Tony Ruddy, thank you for having the vision to create something wonderful.

Thanks to Michael Inch, your food photography has brought so much warmth to this work, and to Carol Mason, my food muse, who has carried me along.

Thanks also to Martin Driscoll, Lisa Ventura, Sian Lenegan, Keith Wootton, Matthew Thornton-Brown and Rosemarie Sellers for their ongoing support, it is much appreciated.

Love and thanks to all my family here and in India who have unearthed so many gems in the form of photographs and stories and offered such support.

Thank you to my husband, Vijay and daughter, Anya, who understood the importance of the project and gave me the love, space, time and support to complete it.

My thanks also go to Shona Charlton, London, www.flickr.com/photos/dark_rain/ for supplying the pictures of Old Delhi in Chapter Two and to Gurpreet Singh Sanghera and the Sanghera family for supplying the pictures of Bilga in Chapter Three, www.bilga.tv

Ever since mum was diagnosed with
Motor Neurone Disease (MND), our
family has been helped and supported
in so many different ways.

The moral and practical support from
health care workers has been exemplary,
as has the support of the of the charity
the MND Association. We are very
grateful to all those involved in her care.

A proportion of the proceeds of this book
will be donated to the MND Association

Registered Charity Number 294354.

Notes

Notes

Notes

Notes